5 Key Skills
to Transform
the Way
You Lead

LEARN2 Lead

Creating Campus Leaders from the Inside-Out

Jeff Stafford

To the hall directors, advisors and student affairs
professionals who shape the life and leadership
of students daily.

This book is dedicated to your efforts, your passions
and your enthusiasm in creating the
TOTAL student experience.

I know for me, if it weren't for a tap on the shoulder to
join hall council and be the travel chair for UUB as an
undergrad at Western Illinois University, who knows
where this student affairs educator might be today.

And to all the students in leadership roles – grab on,
enjoy the ride because this time is preparing you
to step into the role of your life.

CONTENTS

Introduction

1 Language   17
2 Enthusiasm   33
3 Attitude   49
4 Relationships   64
5 Now   79

Be   95

ACKNOWLEDGMENTS

Leadership is not an act done alone – nor was this book.

During the development of this book, I had a chance to reconnect and rekindle some relationships with student affairs professionals I worked with over the years. They dedicated their time, energy and brainpower to help me shape – and complete – this book. I really appreciate the feedback and ideas. Every leader needs a solid group or team – and I was fortunate enough to have this group be part of what I consider my team in bringing these ideas to students.

LeeAnn Melin – I'll never forget the NODA planning team, or the "chance" meeting on the street that turned into some really great chances to work together. You're a truly an amazing gift to student development. Thanks for being part of this development.

Aarin Distad – Internally grateful for you throwing my name into the ring to work with your students. I've enjoyed the collaboration in working with you (and your students) as well as your thoughtful approach in sharing your ideas and thoughts.

T.Todd Masman – Your feedback and thoughts to this – and other! – projects is much appreciated. I'm looking forward to the day we show up to another conference and get to have some real, in person conversation. Thanks for always taking the time to lend your input.

Karen Lohr – from student leader to student affairs professional; you've been a total champion of mine and I so appreciate it. This "fish guy" is always willing to lend a helping hand.

Troy Campbell – You raised the bar to engage me to be really conscious of the meaning I wanted to create through my word choice.

Eric Johnson – WOWZA!!! You helped bring total life to this book. From editing to layout to design. You also bring life to my life. More than I can say thank you!

BRING JEFF TO CAMPUS

Jeff's engaging energy and contagiously positive approach create a life-changing event for people.

Whether it's a student leader training or a student development retreat – attendees will feel their earth tilt on its axis by the end of the session, as they look forward to deeper connections and stronger relationships at work and in their lives.

Participants experience learning in new and different ways. In an OST workshop, there is something for everyone

- Active Participation
- Small Group Conversation
- Lots of Laughing & Learning together
- Hands-on Engagement

Some of Jeff's most popular programs include:

- LEARN2 Lead – based on his recent book
- Unleash Your Inner Super Hero
- Surfing the Waves of Change
- Being 100% Accountable
- Ignite the Creative Leader Within

Call Jeff to discuss what's possible for you when you bring Orange Slice Training to campus.
612-670-0353
www.OrangeSliceTraining.com

"Create the memories of your future today."

— Jeff Stafford

Intro

Why another book on leadership?

I was once myself a student leader on campus and there were many times I felt like I was doing all the work. I felt alone and disconnected from the other students. I first saw it as APATHY, their apathy, and their inability to step up, jump in, and get involved.

It took a while, but I finally realized it was me! My leadership style was what needed a jolt. Other students weren't apathetic – my leadership style was pathetic! So I decided to change that.

Later, as a Director of Campus Life, charged with creating leadership programs for students, I wanted to make sure we could combat the #1 reason why students don't get involved. Not apathy, but less than terrific leadership.

> **It's tempting for leaders to take on too much of the responsibility.**

True leadership engages others

It's tempting for leaders to take on too much of the responsibility and not allow others to contribute. It might seem like it's quicker to do it yourself, but it really isn't. It's less effective and it's lonely!

One of the goals of this book is to provide you and your organization with tools to engage others – that's the true essence of leadership. When leaders learn this, the problem of apathy also seems to take care of itself. In turn, change occurs on campus when groups, not just leaders, take on the challenge of changing the campus community.

True leadership engages others to participate fully in the game of campus life. Being able to teach leaders the skills that produce great programs, provide opportunities for themselves to learn and grow, and ENGAGE others on campus is what I was up to as a Director of Student Life.

I'm STILL up to that!

Through speaking, training and coaching, I guide campus leaders to really dig in, get real about their leadership and harness their Super Powers for good!

This book is a result of the working (and learning!) I have been doing with campuses across the country over the last 15 years, with student leaders, incoming students and even staff working on college campuses.

The 5 Core Skills of Great Leaders

I've identified 5 core skills to master as leaders. They are the skills of: Language, Enthusiasm, Attitude, Relationship, and Now.

I call these five words skills in the hopes of providing an active context that shapes the way you transform leadership into a way of being. I want to turn some simple nouns into action words that can be expressed through our leadership. Through actions that impact the greater good of campus life.

It's in that context I have created a new way to view each skill as it relates to campus leadership. In the end leadership is a way of being. An Action.

This book is a guide that supplements the learning you have done up to this point in the area of leadership development. Use it as a springboard to set you and your organization apart from the others. And by all means, use it as a tool to recruit, retain and renew others touched by your leadership efforts.

Make college a JUICY time

College is a great time in our lives, a colleague of mine calls it a "learning laboratory." I call it a juicy time. Experimenting with new approaches, combining new concepts and ideas in the experiment of your life and your leadership!

Being involved on campus opens you up to so many opportunities that not only provide you the challenge of growing your leadership skills, but offers up support and encouragement to do this in an environment where mistakes can be seen as learning.

Thomas Edison first learned 3,000 ways how not to make a lightbulb. It wasn't until that 3,001 time a new one was allowed to shine. Practice. Get really good at taking risks, tripping up and maybe even having some big juicy flops. This is the time to learn. Let your leadership light shine bright in this experiment.

There is an ever growing focus towards a more intrinsic and heartfelt approach to leadership.

Most of all, use this framework as a way to BE in the world. Doing so is going to create amazing experiences that bring to light the kind of life you want to live – and the type of leader you want to be. For today – and for the days in which college is just an amazingly delicious memory you get to relive with old friends. Trust me on this one. Create those great memories today!

Student Leadership for the New World

We are in a time in which the climate on campus – and out in the world – is changing. There is an ever growing focus towards a more intrinsic and heartfelt approach to leadership. Brain science and positive psychology are shaping the way leaders lead in the world, with a greater attention being paid to the softer skills in life.

These are the same skills that contribute to community building as a way to change the world – the New World. It's an amazing time now when CEO's of major corporations are taking time to think about how their emotional intelligence, not just their cognitive intelligence, might actually influence – or detract from – their success. This is a new way of thinking about how leaders can be successful.

The fact that you are reading this book is shifting your perspective and view of traditional leadership and positioning you to help change the way in which our culture defines leadership. A way that will bring us closer together while positively impacting our community and those around us.

The idea that leadership is not about the position you hold, or the title you have, is a fundamental belief for success in this New World. If no one cares to follow your lead; you're not a leader. Just because you bang the gavel; you're not a leader. Leaders are made from character, insights and the actions they bring forth.

> **The leader of today is a creator and collaborator.**

Leadership in this New World is an active and intentional way of being. Something that engages more than just the rational mind, but also the compassionate heart and desire to build strong relationships and community on campus.

How to Use this Book

This simple book provides you a framework to better define and create Leadership for this New World. The leader of today is a creator and collaborator. They create not just with the words they use, but the actions that follow.

> **Great leaders acknowledge others.**

I invite you to use this book, like a Playbook. Learn the lessons along the way. Take the opportunities to practice the skills from each chapter. At the end of each chapter there is a section I call, Build the Muscle. This is where you get to train and practice using this skill. Just like great athletes need to hit the gym, great leaders need to hit the campus and practice.

Use the exercises to increase your self awareness of how you lead as well as identify what you might do to enhance your current leadership style. At the end of each chapter is also a Celebrate Your Success page – be sure to complete this. The importance of celebrating allows you to pause and reflect on your accomplishments. Too often, I jump to "continuous improvement mode" and forget to do this myself. Great leaders acknowledge others – so take the time here to get good at acknowledging your own efforts.

You might use this with your Advisor, or even the other leaders in your organization. But, by all means raise the checkered flag, take the victory lap and high-five each other along the way for the great efforts you are contributing to the campus experience for yourself – and others! Participating in this act of celebration allows you to notice the changes you are implementing and reminds you of what can occur when you put your focus towards something big in life.

Beliefs

Before diving in, I offer up a few key beliefs that will help this material get deep in your bones and truly transform your leadership style:

> I believe I can make a difference in my campus community one action at a time.
>
> I believe that I have the courage to stand for something greater than myself.
>
> I believe I have what it takes to lead others successfully.
>
> I also believe that I am open to being a leader of integrity, compassion and commitment.

It's within these core beliefs your inner leader lives. Throughout your journey I encourage you to summon up that leader and let the light shine bright. I encourage you to let yourself play BIG and to go after what you really want.

I also encourage you to laugh – and to learn! – along the way.

"**Act as if it were impossible to fail.**"

\- Dorothea Brande

Language

" For me, words are a form of action, capable of influencing change. "

\- Ingrid Bengis

1.
Language

Your words create your world

It's something you do every day. For most of us, not a day goes by when we don't get into a conversation with someone else. And in the off chance you're isolated out in the woods on a retreat by yourself – you probably are having a conversation in your head, with you.

The **Language** we choose to create conversation – either with ourselves or each other – is one of the most powerful choices we can make. Sometimes we choose words unconsciously and without intention of what we are trying to create. Think of some of the great leaders in history and the words they chose to inspire others, to lead with, or to live by. Who comes to mind for you?

> **It's through language Dr. King created a belief for others. A sense of hope**.

You can't mention speech and language and not think of Dr. Martin Luther King, Jr. Using intentional and powerful word choice, he created a message that spawned a movement. It was through his thoughtful delivery of the **Language** that he was able to change people's minds, thoughts, beliefs – and ultimately behaviors. Going back to his *I Have a Dream* speech, his deliberately chosen words created a movement and inspired a generation of people to do something different.

It's through **Language** Dr. King created a belief for others. A sense of hope. His vision inspired others to a more inclusive community, one where everyone could feel they belong and are valued. People felt empowered just listening to the **Language** of his leadership.

Now, you don't need to be the next MLK, you just need to recognize the ability you have to shape your leadership through **Language**.

So, what are you creating from the words you use – with yourself and your group? This is a powerful piece because most leaders pride themselves on being "problem solvers" and tackling the problems. Shift it a bit. What might occur if you started to **Language** your conversations around the solutions you want to create rather than the problems you'd like to have vanish?

What Are You Talking About?

You may have heard of the Law of Attraction. It was made popular in the mainstream through the book and movie *The Secret*. There is science to support the benefits of **Language** as it relates to success.

Our brains are very effective organs, they want to find evidence to support the thoughts we have. For example, if you choose to say, "Today is the worst day of my life" guess what – your brain wants to find evidence to support that thought. You will find ways in which, yes, today is the worst day of your life.

> **Your brain wants to find evidence to support that thought.**

Now the same thing happens when you **Language** it differently. "Today is the best day of my life." Your brain is activated and goes on its journey to collect evidence in support of your statement. We start to notice want we want. Worst or Best. You will find things to support your **Language**.

As leaders, do you want more solutions? Or problems? It's an easy answer, and an easy shift when you start to harness your **Language** and create the solutions through the words you give to them.

Inclusive language

Your words don't just create solutions; they give life to your style and beliefs as a leader. Leading a meeting and saying, "You guys get it right?" works great if you're a fraternity president speaking to all your male members. The conscious choice of using inclusive **Language** speaks volumes about your style. Some might just say, "it's just semantics – it doesn't really matter." It matters to that person, or group of people that often find themselves on the fringes and being marginalized. As leaders there can be a consciousness of whether to contribute to marginalizing a group of people, or to be more inclusive. Either way, your words definitely do create meaning.

The Powerful You

The type of leader for the New World is someone who is bold about dreaming the success that can be.

Leaders who create the future, a world of solutions, are powerful leaders. They have an ability that attracts others to want to follow their lead. Imagine yourself following a leader who is always concerned with obstacles and problems. The **Language** they use tends to sound like this: "We really shouldn't" or "We can't because..." or "It's always been done this way, so we better not." Boring. Who wants to follow that?

The type of leader for the New World is someone who is bold about dreaming the success that can be. This is powerful. Here are a few questions you can use with your group to excite and engage – and in turn share the Powerful You that you are becoming as a leader of the group.

What does success look like for us?

If we could do this even better than anticipated, what would we do first?

Who would be the top 5 people on campus that would rally and support our efforts?

What would make (another organization, person, administration) say Yes! to our request?

When we come back for our 10 year reunion, what do we want people to say about our organization?

By simply asking questions that are designed this way, you start to create very different conversations for your organization. These questions are forward thinking and future oriented. Powerful questions, like the ones above, create energy in the group and provide a positive direction in which to come together.

"Whether you say you can, or you say you can't... either way you're right!" - Anonymous

We create a context – a perspective, through our **Language**. It's in the act of declaring something that you as a leader can create possibilities and options for your group. This type of speech can really shift a group or organization. It can also shift the way in which you personally view situations. Because **Language** is an act of creation – a declaration is like a stake in the ground. It marks the territory and creates a claim for you and your group.

> It's through our Language that anything is possible and through our actions that we experience results.

Here's an example – think about the last wedding or commitment ceremony you may have attended. The couple knew each other a while, dated and then they invited you to "their" day. In front of everyone they shared their commitment and love to each other – you as a witness. In the moment they kissed it was different. But, what was really different? Their commitment. It was in this declaration a new union or partnership was created. Different and very much distinguished from the 15 minutes prior to the kiss.

Through declarations we create a way of being. A new context opens up to us.

As leaders of an organization our declarations hold much weight because they provide us the opportunity to walk our talk or stumble and trip. Our actions carry out our declarations. Because we say it to be true – it can be. We just need to live our declarations through our actions. It's through our **Language** that anything is possible and through our actions that we experience results.

If I stand in front of my own group and declare, "This is the best organization on campus!" How does the organization's behavior change when this is their paradigm? All of a sudden they may start to act differently, expect more of themselves and others. It is not just the leader, but the power of the group. There are so many options and choices of what actions to take to live this new reality. Nothing external needs to change. The actions right at this moment start to support my declaration.

Setting the Tone

As leaders you are capable of helping set the tone and style of the organization. Tone can be a predictor of the success an organization will have in the coming year. Leaders who become more self aware of **Language** can really set and shift the tone of the group – and ultimately shift the campus community. Below are a four key phrases that help shift the context and set a tone that contributes to collaboration and relationship building in a group:

Instead of this...	Use this...
But...	Yes, and...
How are you going to do that?	What ways might you go about doing that?
Why...	What if...
That won't work.	We could do that, what other ways might we also try it?

Using **Language** as a leadership tool provides a method to allow others to be involved and engaged. It opens up new contexts and possibilities that attracts new members and retain current ones. As you lead, use **Language** as tool to engage in the important work you and your organization want to be known for. Being purposeful and intentional in asking powerful questions, providing answers and eliciting feedback is a skill that will not only serve you on campus, but for the rest of your life.

 ## Build the Muscle

For the next five days, I invite you to notice how your **Language** impacts your conversations. Go into your conversations as a curious explorer and see possibility and success. Use **Language** to create. Substitute some of the *Instead of this phrases* with the *Use this phrases* and see what difference it has in your conversations. Notice the impact it might have on the success of your organization and relationships you cultivate with members of your group.

" We have more possibilities available in each moment than we realize. "

- Thich Nhat Hanh

Celebrate Your Success

What actions did you take this week? What impact does this have on your campus?

What have you noticed by focusing on using **Language** as a leadership tool?

What successes have you had as a result of your focus this week?

What was different for you this week?

How might you fine tune the leadership skill of using **Language** to become an even stronger leader than you are today?

What does successfully mastering this skill look like for you?

Who might be able to help you in this effort?

Notes and reflections

"**When you discover your mission, you will feel its demand. It will fill you with enthusiasm and a burning desire to get to work on it.**"

– W. Clement Stone

Enthusiasm

"**Enthusiasm is contagious. Be a carrier.**"

- Susan Rabin

2.
Enthusiasm

We have about 30 seconds to make a first impression. What kind of first impression do you make? Effective leaders demonstrate the type of energy you can't help but want to be around. Someone who has the ability to exude this type of energy is someone who is passionate about what they are doing.

There is an alignment with your inner self that is so contagious others are attracted to what you are putting out. By demonstrating our **Enthusiasm** for a cause, a group, or a change on campus we have the ability to attract people to want to be involved.

> **It's that authentic enthusiasm and excitement that draws others to be involved with our organizations.**

Enthusiasm is your soul shining through

I'm not advocating you plaster on a smile and bounce around campus – unless that is truly who you are at the core. I am inviting you to let your true self, your inner child we all have, out for others to see. You know the one, the one who gets so excited about going to Disneyland that you can't sleep the night before.

It's that authentic enthusiasm and excitement that draws others to be involved with our organizations. As a campus speaker, I've had people come up to me after workshops and talks and say, "You must really love what you do." I tell them I do, and ask, "What makes you say that?" "It's how you talk about it – (leadership, goal setting, or whatever the topic was that evening) – you get so excited. I can see it really matters to you."

It does! It's that undeniable belief in what I'm doing matters that allows **Enthusiasm** to just seep out of my pores. You can't help but get a little bit on you – in a good way!

Leadership in the New World is about being excited, passionate and approachable. This doesn't mean to show up in the "jump around" sense, just however you truly express interest and enthusiasm. Gone are the days when a successful leader needs to put up the walls around them and be stoic. You know the walls – the ones where you know all the answers and there is a big divide between leader and the pack. This doesn't work on campus and it's not going to suit you well beyond college either.

Science now tells us...

Research into brain science is allowing us to understand more about behavior and how to lead. I have modeled the principles in this book to mirror that of what the research is suggesting. Your **Enthusiasm** is giving people an opportunity to feel a reward when working with you – not to be threatened by your work. Our brain is wired to go into either a reward or threat state, and when we enter the state of threat we don't collaborate, can't solve problems as effectively, and diminish our creativity (*Neuroleadership Journal*, 2008).

> **Your Enthusiasm is giving people an opportunity to feel a reward when working with you**

Great leaders on campus jump at the opportunity to collaborate, think creatively about solutions and have a desire to create something big on campus. That's **Enthusiasm**!

An Extension of Belief

Enthusiasm is an extension of your belief. If you are not passionate, or excited, about something why would I follow you? When leaders speak with belief about the work they are doing you can see it in their eyes, hear it in their tone of voice and it seeps out in the way in which they go about getting others involved.

There is such an internal connection – even drive – when great leaders believe in what they do. Leaders become unstoppable when they have that fire, that belief, in their belly. It's contagious – and so worth catching!

A simple way of demonstrating belief and **Enthusiasm** is to have a very clear connection to your values. When these are known – really known –

you show up in a way that is undeniably you. It's through this expression that **Enthusiasm** oozes. It's the invitation for others to join you in your journey – because it seems like so much fun.

Values guide us through the sometimes difficult decisions we need to make as leaders. Values also influence the actions we choose to take. We become a walking billboard of what's most important to us. This is attractive. When someone is so clear on what they are up to in life, this has the

> **A simple way of demonstrating belief and Enthusiasm is to have a very clear connection to your values.**

potential to draw people closer. And in all honesty, it has the ability to keep away those that don't support us, or the causes we champion.

Values allow an organization to move in the direction of success. To discover and bring about the values your organization pose these three questions:

1. What's the purpose of our organization?
2. What are the characteristics our "ideal members" embody?
3. How do we want to go about living our mission in a way that impacts the greater good of our campus community?

These questions are a primer to create clarity around what the organizations truly values. When an organization is clear about the values they hold true the easier it is to align the efforts, or the members, to bring this about. Values influence decisions, priorities and determine the course of action to take.

I know this to be true for myself. A couple of the values that influenced me greatly in starting Orange Slice Training were Fun, Humor and Choice. This trio of values influences me every day and allows me to serve others in a way that contributes to a greater good.

When I get to work with a group of student leaders, or business professionals, I show up in a way that embodies those three values. I also design leadership experiences and workshops where these are going to be overtly present. I remember one conversation with a group of business leaders who wanted a presentation where I would tell their group what it took to be successful instead of involving them in the conversation of what it means to be successful. It's as if choice was taken from the group and they were there to do what I was going to tell them. I know, through experience, that a group can generate ideas to be successful. I also know that they would be more likely to follow their own ideas rather than a list I created for them.

> **Your values shape your beliefs into the actions you take today and in the future.**

They also wanted me to avoid using the word "Play" in a workshop I was designing because they didn't have time to play and needed to be professional (duh, Fun and Humor are core – and BTW these values can be present and still allow us to be professional and productive!). And, they wanted me to use a podium (ain't gonna work – too much energy needing to get out for me to just stand in one place for 90-minutes).

There was such a fundamental mismatch here that all the Fun and lightheartedness would be sucked out of the room. Fortunate enough for me, we were still in the planning phase when their requests came about. I passed on this opportunity and recommended a colleague that I thought would be a much better fit for what they were looking for.

Your values shape your beliefs into the actions you take today and in the future.

Creating Something Worth Seeing

Leaders need to help a group set a direction, one that aligns with their mission. I suggest involving the group to help paint the vision for the future of the organization. Great leaders also inspire their group towards the vision they have helped create. One of the most essential questions that get members involved in vision setting is a question I threw at you during the Language chapter of this book. *What does success look like?*

This single question propels groups forward to think about the future of the organization, a project or campus event. Using Language is a skill that helps create and gives life to the vision of your organization. In my book, *Create Your Juicy Life*, I designed an exercise to help people create a change in their life – it serves the same purpose as the vision you create with your organization. It's "Creating the Memories of Your Future" and I invite you to use it with your group to share the **Enthusiasm** you have for the organization and help to craft the vision of its future.

Creating the Memories of Your Future

1 **Ask the group** – What do we really want to have happen this year? This is about creating, not avoiding. What change do we want to see on campus as a result of our efforts this year? Increased awareness for our cause, greater student involvement or pride, a stronger sense of community – whatever it is, say it out loud.

2 **Determine the strengths of your group** – What do we do best that is easy and effortless? Get really specific and brag a bit about the group's success. Ask your group – How can we use our strengths to help us achieve what we really want to have happen this year?

3 **Invite Emotions in to cement the vision** – When we have achieved our vision, what will it feel like? List all of the emotions you'd experience as a result of doing the great you we do. Emotions are typically one word in nature (i.e. Proud, Confident, Encouraged, etc.). We tend not to share these, but instead share our cognitive thoughts about what we are feeling. By identifying the emotion, we are creating a greater sense of awareness and increasing our emotional intelligence. Both are key to a leader's success.

Doing this exercise with your group encourages the forward momentum because it starts to answer, "Why are we doing this?" The vision that is created is something to keep revisiting with the group – keeping track to determine whether or not your actions match with what you are hoping to accomplish.

It's also a spark to remind people how they might feel as a result of accomplishing the vision of the organization. This will be especially critical to bring out during mid-terms or high stress weeks on your campus when the last thing someone wants to do is go to another club or organization meeting. Help your group rediscover and recommit their efforts to the group's shared vision.

Lastly, when groups engage in this type of activity – *Creating the Memories of Your Future* – you get to live this today by the actions you take. The vision doesn't have to be a destination point; it's about today.

"Enthusiasm releases the drive to carry you over obstacles and adds significance to all you do."

- Norman Vincent Peale

Build the Muscle

This week use your **Enthusiasm** to engage group members and allow your values to shine through.

You might check in with your Career Services office on campus to see if they offer a workshop or tool to help you determine your Top 5 values if you haven't done this before. Print out your Top 5 and carry them with you – you might even put them on the back of your student ID, something you have with you all the time. This week, practice making choices that are in alignment with your values. We tend to do this subconsciously, but make the shift this week to be super-intentional about your choices and allow your **Enthusiasm** and belief to shine through.

Celebrate Your Success

What actions did you take this week? What impact does this have on your campus?

How has your **Enthusiasm** shaped your actions this week? How has it helped you lead more effectively?

What successes have you had as a result of your focus this week?

What was different for you this week?

What does successfully mastering the skill of **Enthusiasm** look like for you?

Who might be able to help you in this effort?

Notes and reflections

"If you don't like something, change it. If you can't change it, change your attitude. "

- Maya Angelou

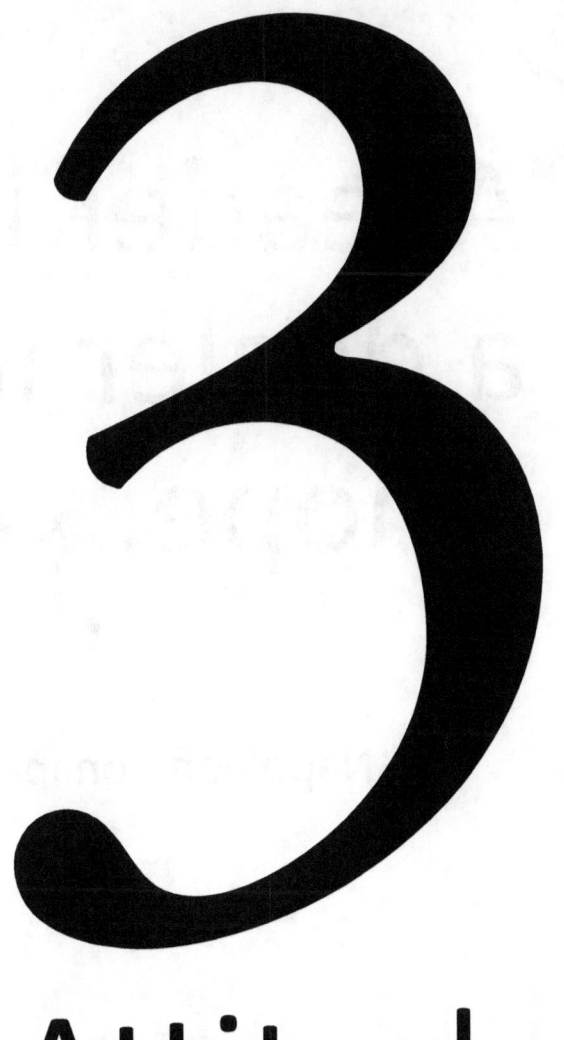

Attitude

"A leader is a dealer in hope."

— Napoleon Bonaparte

3.
Attitude

The potential that we have as leaders is greatly influenced by the **Attitude** we choose. There are times in which I wake up on the "wrong side of the bed" or run late into a meeting. Believe me, I'm just like you.

Everything is not always roses and lollipops. Yet, I also know how I decide to show up influences whether or not people want to be a part of something I am creating. Being able to use **Attitude** as a tool to becoming more effective on campus is a skill to quickly develop.

It's A Simple Choice

> **Attitude is that outward expression of how we choose to let others see us.**

Attitude is that outward expression of how we choose to let others see us. Notice the most important word in the sentence – choose. Have you ever given any thought to what you absolutely control in life? Really, absolutely – no influence from someone else making you, pushing you, thrusting you to do or own something.

The only thing that I can come up with is **Attitude**. Yep. That's it. **Attitude**. The only thing. Sure, you might be thinking, but … people make me have the **Attitude** I have. Between whatever action they have done – or not done (i.e. didn't call you back when they said they would) and your **Attitude** is this delicious space called Choice. So, what do you do in this space? Get Mad. Upset. Tickled. What happens for you in this space called Choice?

This space is wide open with possibilities. In the midst of nothing, there is something for you to create. A true, honest and authentic Choice. Herein lies the key to becoming an effective leader on campus – the real you gets to show up here. This isn't customer service 101 where you have to have a 3 ¼ inch smile and where the phrase "fake it 'til you make it!" lives. This is where the real you gets to glow and be big. Real. Authentic. Choice. It's in that space we have options. Options to create anything we want.

Does My Choice Support My Goals?

When I worked with my team of orientation leaders during summer Welcome Days, **Attitude** was a key factor for our success. After 18 hours, in the hot days of August working together with swarms of family members and ever-questioning new students, **Attitude** was going to keep us on track. It was important for us to remember the Vision and goals we created for our program. When we could recall those, we could also be in a better place to choose the **Attitude** that was going to support our success.

> **People enjoy working with others that take responsibility for their actions.**

Our goal was to create a really great place in which both students and their families were excited to come back to in the fall. We also wanted people to know we were sincerely grateful that they chose us. With that in mind, we could show up in ways to support that – a smile, seeing opportunity and being excited to connect and share information. When the goals are clear the action to take is easy to see.

Taking Charge of Yourself

After noticing how much **Attitude** influenced my ability to develop positive relationships and get things done, I started to leverage this as a very conscious tool to use. A colleague of mine said to me, "Jeff, you always seem to be in a positive mood; do you ever have bad days?" As I told you, yes even I do wake up on the wrong side of the bed at times. But I don't let it dictate my day. When you execute the choice you want to make with your **Attitude**, you start to take charge of the actions you do.

No one is making you do anything; there is a choice there. You get to be in control. People enjoy working with others that take responsibility for their actions. It also lets others know they aren't going to suddenly be blamed for something that wasn't their fault. Being accountable creates

"The state of your life is nothing more than a reflection of the state of your mind."

- Wayne Dyer

trust and safety in groups. When groups have a strong sense of trust, great relationships form. It's during those times of stress – the 18-hour days during Orientation – when a great relationship is the one thing that is going to allow me to support you and help us get things done.

Build the Muscle

This week start each day by creating the intention for what **Attitude** will help you get through your day most successfully. Write this **Attitude** on a note card and take it with you to class, meetings or work. Use it as a reminder to keep focused on the goal you have and how your **Attitude** can help you accomplish that, versus taking you away from what you want.

Celebrate Your Success

What actions did you take this week? What impact does this have on your campus?

How has your **Attitude** shaped your actions this week? How has it helped you lead more effectively?

What successes have you had as a result of your focus this week?

What was different for you this week?

What does successfully mastering the skill of **Attitude** look like for you?

Who might be able to help you in this effort?

"Happiness is an attitude. We either make ourselves miserable, or happy and strong. The amount of work is the same."

- Francesca Reigler

Notes and reflections

"When we seek to discover the best in others, we somehow bring out the best in ourselves."

- William Arthur Ward

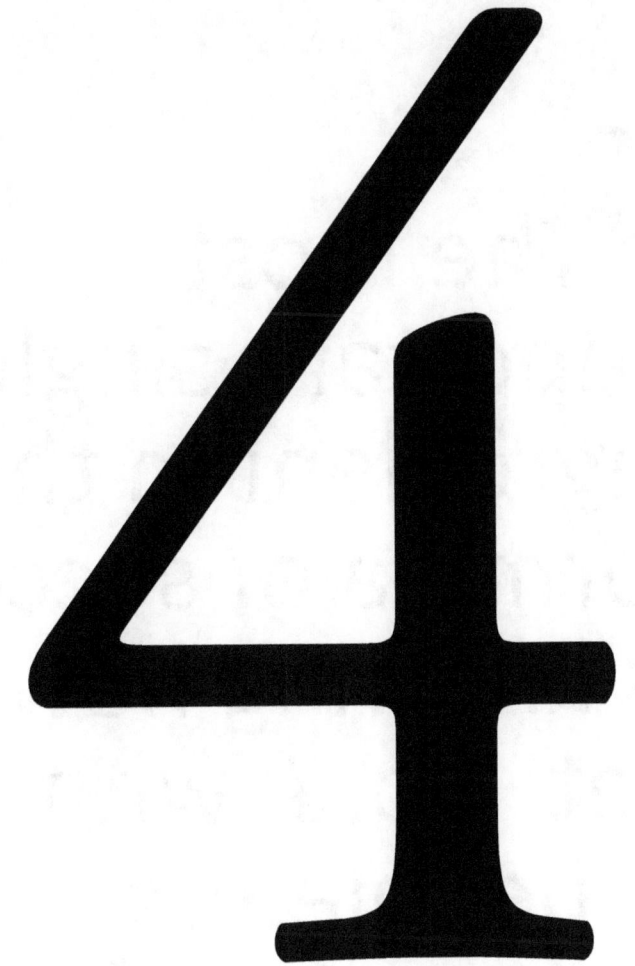

Relationships

"**The most important single ingredient in the formula of success is knowing how to get along with people.**"

- Theodore Roosevelt

4.
Relationships

W e need others to help us move the vision forward. We don't live in a world where we can interact solely with ourselves and have a productive and satisfying life. Even Facebook relies on us having some sort of a relationship – or connection – with others. Good **Relationships** are important for groups to function well and achieve success.

The Start Up

E arly on in a group's development, attention needs to be paid to the relationship of the group members. Often times, leaders want to jump in and get going on the task at hand, the event that needs to be planned, or the rally that is occurring. However, if you have not struck the right balance between task and relationship you are running the risk of disaster later on. And losing members of the group.

Taking time to get to know each other beyond the group will be essential to call on when the group starts working together.

Taking time with your group to get to know each other and the interests they have that extend beyond the group will be essential to call on when the group starts working together. That interest in others also gives you a glimpse into what motivates people to be involved with your organization rather than spending their time elsewhere.

Try out the questions on the following page to create deeper **Relationships** with your members and peek into what motivates them to be involved with your group.

What's one thing you hope to accomplish by being involved?

If money were no object, how would you spend your time? What brings a smile to your face and a pep to your step?

How does the mission of our organization overlap with the some of your core values?

If we were to be really successful planning our next event, how would you like to celebrate?

What's something you love to do just for fun?

What do you like best about _____? (weekends, your major, the college)

These are questions you can use at your next meeting – cut them up and have people draw them out of a hat and have the entire group answer.

Effective leaders will spend more energy during the start up phase on relationship than task.

You might even include one in your agenda for meetings as a check-in item at the start to kick off your meeting. You might think you don't have time for this – in fact you're not alone, many managers in organizations buy into this myth. Then when conflict arises, they spend ten times the amount of energy repairing and rebuilding the **Relationships** they ignored in the beginning of their team development.

As a former Director of Campus Life it was important for me to take groups like the Programming Board, Student Government, or Orientation Leaders on overnight retreats when possible. We needed to get away, spend some time together planning for the future of the organization or program. And we also needed to really bond and get to know each other.

Effective leaders will spend more energy during the start up phase on relationship than task. This builds trust and commitment to the group. Over time, the effort can shift to managing task because the group is strong and has developed effective ways to communicate and handle differences. The leadership of the organization can then focus on the results they expect to deliver to the campus community.

Your Inner Circle

I think it's funny how we develop during college. I say this now, because it has come full circle and played itself out for me. We get to college and seek our independence – to be on our own. We need to learn these things – to cook, clean, do laundry; all the fun things that seem to just happen when I lived at home. Then we go out and we are on our own and there can be this great sense of pride and confidence that comes with this too. And sometimes this confidence fools us, that to be on our own we must do it alone. Bzzzzzzzzzzzzz. Wrong answer. Independence yes, alone no.

> **Celebrate the relationship you have with those to be considered in your Inner Circle**

I've developed an exercise that I use with groups to demonstrate how we can call on our connections and relationships to help us be even more effective as leaders, it's called "Your Inner Circle." In indigenous cultures, there are tribes of people who live together, harvesting the land and ultimately looking out for the success of others. Collaboration, rather than competition, is valued. The Inner Circle honors family tribes in a way that demonstrates the need for connection to our success as leaders.

I've included the worksheet at the end of this book. Here are the instructions for completing it.

1 Put your name in the middle of the target.

2 In the second ring, put the names of those you consider to be in your inner circle. Who are you proud to have in this group? Who, if they were not present in your life, would leave a big gap?

3 In the outer ring, identify all the things/thoughts/beliefs your Inner Circle provides for you. They probably are so good at providing it they might not even know it landed on your list.

And if you really want to have the skill of **Relationships** at the core of your leadership style, you'll connect and let them know they are in your Inner Circle and support you. Give them a call and tell them WHY. Connect. Meaningfully, with intention and with the love in your heart that they gift you by showing up as part of your Inner Circle.

You can do this with your organization as well. Use flip chart paper to design your own wall-size "Your Inner Circle" worksheet. Put a picture of your group in the middle circle and draw the two outer rings. In the second ring identify those who support your organization. This might be other groups on campus you collaborate with, administrators who support (and fund!) your organization, or people you turn to when you need a jolt of energy. In the third ring, do the same as you did for your personal worksheet and identify how they contribute to your organization.

Through your organization that there is potential to impact a community long after you have graduated

End the exercise with creating ways in which to celebrate the relationship you have with those to be considered in your Inner Circle. Honor them. Thank them. Most of all connect with them. Being able to recognize your Inner Circle acknowledges you don't do this alone.

We vs. Me Mentality

As a leader, you play an important role on campus. Yet it is through your organization that there is potential to impact a community long after you have graduated. Creating a legacy that is focused around the efforts of the group is much more sustainable – and palatable – than a legacy focused on you as the leader. It's shifting the focus from "Me" to "We." Sure you might be the Student Government President who got the funding for a new ice cream machine in your residence hall. But, how powerful could the change be if what had your focus was to create something larger, like the legacy of your group.

This shift in focus drives the activity of the group today. The group you lead helps create the legacy they want to leave for others in the future. You have the ability to shape a transformation that can be sustained by shifting the spotlight to the group. You also encourage others to join you on stage as you create the legacy together. It's easier to get people moving in the same direction when they too can shape the future. (Revisit the chapters on **Language**, **Enthusiasm** and **Attitude** if you want hints on doing this effectively.)

Shifting the focus of how the group will live on, rather than how you as a leader survives, creates the type of legacy you want to leave behind.

"I suppose leadership at one time meant muscles; but today it means getting along. with people."

– Gandhi

Build the Muscle

This week set your intention on really connecting with your group members and allowing them opportunities to connect with each other. Try to keep a scorecard of at least one new thing you learned about each of your group members. For a more advanced routine, try to find out the internal motivation for people to become even more active and involved in your group. This will take some keen listening and questioning skills. Once you get this information – use it!

 **Celebrate Your Success**

What actions did you take this week? What impact does this have on your campus?

How has the skill of **Relationships** shaped your actions this week? How has it helped you lead more effectively?

What successes have you had as a result of your focus this week?

What was different for you this week?

What does successfully mastering the skill of **Relationships** look like for you?

Who might be able to help you in this effort?

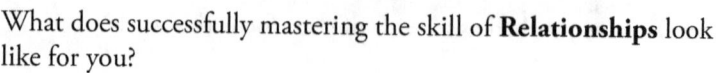

Notes and reflections

Notes and reflections

" How we
spend our days is,
of course,
how we spend
our lives. "

- Annie Dillard

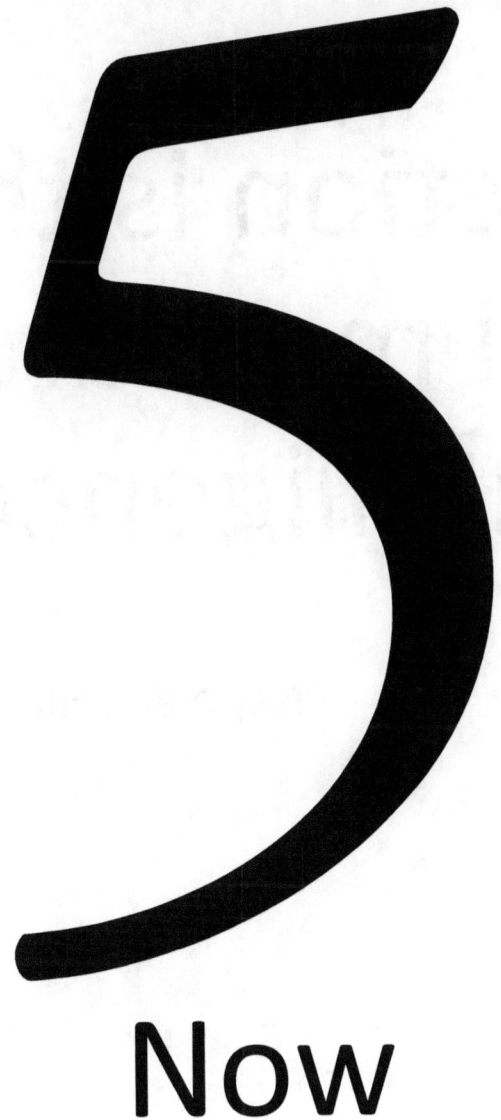

Now

"**Action is the real measure of intelligence.**"

- Napolean Hill

5.
Now

All of what you have been reading and practicing about leadership for this New World does no good unless there is action. The power of **Now** is excitedly important to the impact your group has on the campus community. It's the ability to walk the walk and not just provide the talk of a good game. It's about being real and living in the moment that generates success and brings people together for the greater good.

Being Here

One of the fundamental skills I remember teaching my Orientation Leaders was the skill of being present and in the moment. During Welcome Days when hundreds of new family members and students descended upon campus, it was important to stay focused. While we would see a number of different sessions, the student and their family only had ONE orientation experience and we were going to make it dynamite!

The ability to recognize when you slip from the present moment to the mind-altering thoughts that day dreams are made of, is an important first step. The next step is then getting back to the **Now**. As leaders it's important to truly be able to turn off the background noise and allow members to know that you are present. Members perceive this as you caring for them – and that you value their time. Both of these lead to the glue that holds groups together – TRUST. (You might remember that from the chapter on Relationships.)

Taking Action

I've done a number of different workshops on Goal Setting and Strategic Visioning with groups across the country. When it comes time to setting an action plan in place, sometimes people feel handcuffed like they can't move and get anything done. I remember when things like Homecoming, Graduation, or Welcome Week landed on my to-do list, I too felt handcuffed. The need to really chunk things down is a critical next step in getting something accomplished.

When you are feeling stuck or challenged, ask yourself "what is the next physical action I can take?"

David Allen, author of *Getting Things Done*, coined the phrase I like using with groups – Next Action. What is the physical next action you can take to get something closer to being totally accomplished and off your list? This mental shift creates a focus and an energy to take on most any project you encounter as a leader.

It's through our actions that our talk turns into the walk we walk.

When you are feeling stuck or challenged, ask yourself "what is the next physical action I can take?" This will provide you more than direction, it also will introduce a comfort that can ease the overwhelming feeling we sometimes feel as leaders.

The enVisioned Leader

In the chapter on Enthusiasm I introduced a visioning exercise from my book, *Create Your Juicy Life*. I wanted to provide another exercise from the book that goes a bit deeper into the topic of vision. As a leader one of the primary roles you play is the ability to inspire your members around the vision of your organization.

This exercise invites you to really commit to taking action on being able to create that vision for yourself. I'm going to ask you to do something that has the ability to rewire your brain in ways that will allow you to see your vision come to life by creating some daily habits and actions. Sounds big? It is…because the payoff is HUGE!

To do this, you'll need a few things to be successful:

- A notebook and something to write with
- A spot on campus you really enjoy being at – and some place that will allow you to have about 30-minutes of uninterrupted time
- A mind and imagination that can really think BIG (you've already got this, or you wouldn't be reading this!)

I want you to think about the vision you have for the kind of leader you'd like to become.

Imagine that you and your advisor are having a conversation two years from today. In this conversation both of you are reflecting back on the type of leader you have become. Not only was it easier than you had ever anticipated, you accomplished more with your group and for your campus than what both of you thought was ever be possible. It's with great pride and confidence that you have grown into that leader for the New World.

I invite you to ponder this notion. I want you to step into this vision you have created for yourself and really feel what it's like to have been able to provide this type of leadership. And to be this type of leader.

Now, I invite you to write out a one-page reflection of what took place in the last two years that allowed you and your advisor to have such a memorable conversation on your leadership transformation. Write about it as if it has already happened.

Think about life and what it feels like at this moment of achievement.

Write about it from a positive perspective of what you helped create on campus. And tap into the emotional components associated with your accomplishments. Think about life and what it feels like at this moment of achievement --- not the moments leading up to the achievement, but at the finish line. I imagine there is a big smile and sense of pride... what else is there?

Go ahead – write out one full page, single-sided that captures your enVISION (your ideal future).

Now, this is where science and the brain are going to start to help us answer the question, "How is that going to happen?" Read your one page enVision sheet each day for 30-days in a row. The key here is EVERY DAY. It's just reading! Doing this will create new pathways in the brain. Pathways that start to see – and answer – how this vision can be achievable. Astronauts at NASA need to wear these glasses that invert images and make everything appear upside down. Confusing to the brain when you are trying to fly a rocket in space. And life is like that when we create big visions – confusing to the brain. After 25 to 28 days, the astronauts no longer see the images upside down, they appear normal – right side up. The brain created new pathways to allow this. DON'T MISS THIS…if you take the glasses off during that 28 day period, you need to start over… from day 1.

It is going to cement in your brain so deeply that you will start to experience life differently.

Starting now…read your enVISION sheet you created. And then everyday, for the next 30 days repeat this. During that course of 30 days, notice what starts to pop up for you. Notice what you start paying attention to. Notice what actions you are taking that are getting you closer to the vision you have created for yourself.

This isn't Magic. Poof. Goal Achieved.

It is going to cement in your brain so deeply that you will start to experience life differently. You will take different actions. You will be up for accomplishing this, simply because you took aim. By doing this each day you start to shape today and create actions that you can take **Now**.

Bonus…If you want to take this a step further, find yourself an image and paste it to the back of your enVISION document. Something that stirs up all the positive emotions, greatness and success you will experience as a result of your accomplishment.

Build the Muscle

This week I invite you to play around with two concepts from this chapter. I know you are ready for it because you have made it to this

> " I have been impressed with the urgency of doing. Knowing is not enough; we must apply. Being willing is not enough; we must do. "
>
> — Leonardo da Vinci

point in the program. First, start seeing how the Next Action philosophy of getting things accomplished impacts your results. When you have a task or project to be accomplished for your group – think about what is the next physical action you can take.

Secondly, I want you to notice what starts to show up for you as you read your enVision sheet for the next 30 days. What do you start to see that helps you create the story you've created? Keep track of these in a journal or notebook. This will allow you to see if this exercise has made any difference in the way in which you lead.

Celebrate Your Success

What actions did you take this week? What impact does this have on your campus?

How has the skill of **Now** shaped your actions this week? How has it helped you lead more effectively?

What successes have you had as a result of your focus this week?

What was different for you this week?

What does successfully mastering the skill of **Now** look like for you?

Who might be able to help you in this effort?

Notes and reflections

Notes and reflections

"We're all called. If you're here breathing, you have a contribution to make."

- Oprah Winfrey

Be

"Be the change you want to see in the world."

- Mahatma Gandhi

Be!

Congratulations on getting to this point in the book. I hope you've been able to dig in and explore along the way as you created a stronger sense of self and a greater awareness of how to lead even more effectively in the New World.

In the previous chapters you got to experience some fundamentals to shape campus life through your leadership. In the chapter on Language you started to create awareness around how your choice of words can create the world in which you live. There was an intentionality created to help shift the belief that **Language** is a tool that can inspire others to follow your lead. In the chapter on **Enthusiasm**, you got in touch with what matters most – your values. You allowed yourself to create a vision for your organization – one that is a memory of the future you desire. The chapter on **Attitude** asks you to account for how your choices help you meet your goals.

Leading is not done alone. The chapter on **Relationships** helped you to identify your Inner Circle – the group that supports and champions you. Lastly, you put this all together so that your talk turned into the walk created by the actions you take. It's here that you have started to rewire your brain with the vision for your own leadership on campus.

One last belief I want to offer up is …

Leadership is about Being.

It's in this way of Being that you not only positively effect yourself, but your community. You show up in ways that impact the lives of others. You get to Be someone who finds joy and purpose in what you do. You get to be You!

Be the change you want to see in the world.
-- Mahatma Ghandi

 **Notes and reflections**

Success 101: Planning for your first year of college

For more than 15 years I've helped thousands of students and families make the transition to college. I know from experience that this can be a difficult time – both for the student and the family members.

That's why I created the Success 101 CD program. If you choose to get this program, you will be taking the first steps to creating the success you want during your first year of college. And that's a great first step!

If you could get access to a plan that has helped thousands of students during their first year, wouldn't you want that? Of course you would.

There's no reason to have to figure it out yourself. This 2 CD program takes an inside-out approach to your success in college. You'll walk through a process that helps you create a vision and identify the steps needed to get you that much closer to a dynamite first year.

Coming Soon...

Unleash Your Inner SuperHero!

A student leader's guide to success

This CD program will walk you step-by-step into ways in which to tap into your potential and access the type of successes you desire. This proven method not only will transform your leadership – it can even land you the job of your dreams.

Rave Reviews

Bringing Jeff to campus will not only allow you to offer some top notch training to your group – but it will make you look like a genius! Look what others have said about bringing him to their events:

"I hired Jeff to provide a goal setting keynote presentation for over 600 new students. He was energetic, funny and was able to get his message across in a way that resonated with both new and transfer students."

- Katie Svoboda, Director of Orientation

"I initially brought Jeff to CSUMB to train our Orientation Leaders but discovered he had a wealth of knowledge to offer so I hired him to do four different workshops at our annual Student Leadership Conference."

- Kelly Maily, Coordinator for Leadership Development

"If you desire training that is unique, high energy and inspires the audience to take personal action, I strongly recommend you hire Jeff Stafford and Orange Slice Training."

- Janaya Bagurusi, LISC Program Director

"Throughout the years, Jeff has continually created training environments where uncommon learning promote the well-being of everyone...Jeff helps people experience learning in different ways – through active participation, conversation, fun and experiential activities. After spending time in a training session with Jeff, you feel certain about one thing, life (or work) is going to be better!"

- Andy Halper, National Education Director

"Standing shoulder-to-shoulder with Jeff Stafford, I had the opportunity to witness firsthand what people rave about. His is an engaging blend of affable educator and winning motivator who enrolls his audiences naturally. Jeff has exactly what it takes to make "facilitation" easy, smoothing the progress of discovery, growth, learning and new directions."
- Deena Ebbert, International Speaker for ChartHouse Learning

For more reviews, visit Jeff's YouTube Channel at:
www.YouTube.com/OrangeSliceTraining

Coaching with Jeff

- Have you ever felt like life has a lot more to offer you, but you just can't seem to get it?
- Do you wonder what you want to do when you "grow up?"
- Are you trying to find what you want to do with your life?
- Do you ever talk yourself out of being able to have it all?

If you answered YES to any of these questions – you're just like everyone else. The difference is you can do something about it.

Working with Jeff as your coach allows you to ...

- Move towards your passion and purpose in life
- Develop a sense of confidence as you take on the dreams of your life
- Go for something even bigger than you thought was ever possible.

As your coach I am not here to diagnose, fix and analyze anything. I am here to support, challenge and encourage you to lead your best life and ask ... what's next.

So, what's next?

Jeff offers:

- Quick Start Sessions
- One-time LEARN2 Lead sessions
- On-going student leader sessions that will allow you to unleash your leadership potential.

You'll create the vision and action steps to bring it to life.

Contact Jeff at 612-670-0353 or log on to www.OrangeSliceTraining.com/coaching and get started.

BONUS ACTIVITIES

Here's an activity that you can do on your own, or with your organization. It's a great tracking system to help you achieve the goals that are most important to you.

2Day 2Achieve

Much has been written about goal setting and success. From all that I have read, I've come up with a simple form to help each of us achieve the success we desire. There are 3 elements critical to goal setting and success:

1. **Clarity**. Being able to set your aim and focus on something specific helps you to achieve your result. The more specific, the more likely you are to be successful with achieving your result. First: What do you want? Get yourself really clear on what this is. A deeper question that might be helpful to explore is: Why do I want it?

2. **Chunk it down**. Now, I don't need any study to show me that being able to take bite-sized bits of something is easier to swallow than taking one large bite. When a project is too big, too hairy, too scary - I don't do anything. Chunk your goal down into bite-sized pieces.

3.**Action**. To achieve your results, there needs to be action not just thoughts, not just "trying" (i.e. I'm going to try to do it) - but deliberate actions. What are you doing? What are you doing every day that gets you closer to your goal?

Use the 2Day 2Achieve Worksheet to move you closer to your goal. Action by action, day by day you will start to see what you are doing to create your own success. You can use this form at the beginning of each day to plan out what actions you will take. Or, you can use the form at the end of the day and reflect on what two actions did you take today? Either way, you can't go wrong when you are using this tool.

Just 2 a day. What do you choose? More importantly, what are you getting from the actions you've taken?

Download a full page sample on www.orangeslicetraining.com/ 2day

Attitude Influences Everything

Tune into this Choice-making life you are now creating. Set your SmartPhone, iGadget, or old school alarm clock to go off at 8:27, 1:23 and 4:11.

At these moments make the Choice. Ask yourself, "what is the Attitude that is influencing my moment?" If you don't like your answer, make another Choice! This is where you start to create a habit. Of Noticing. Of Choice-making. Of being You. The Powerful You.

Your Inner Circle Worksheet

from page 67

Download a full page sample on www.orangeslicetraining.com/
innercircle

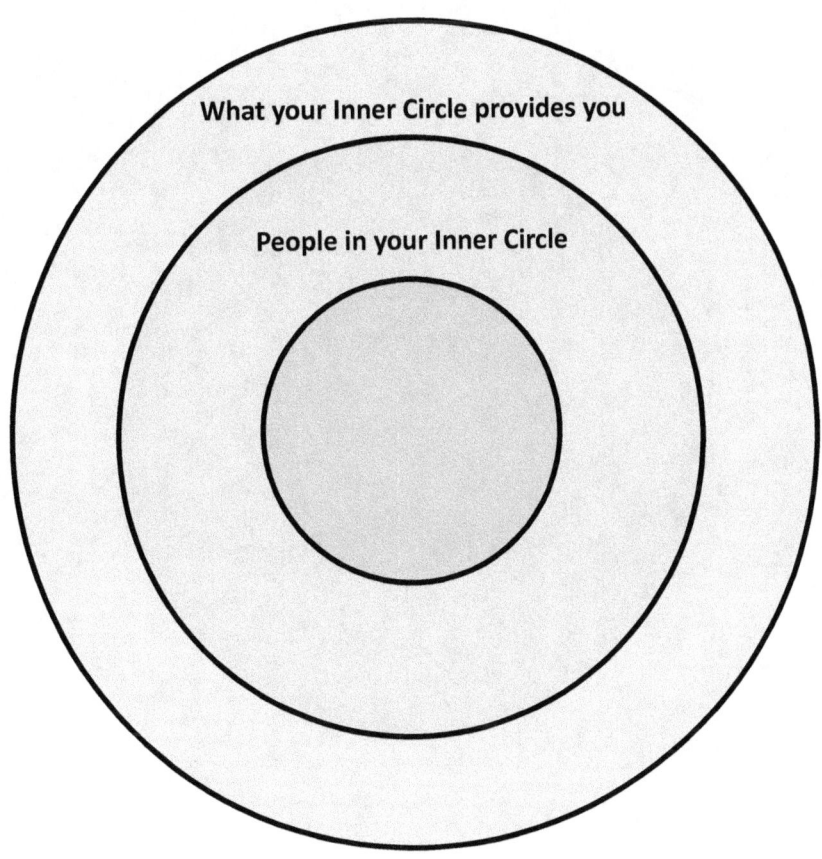

What your Inner Circle provides you

People in your Inner Circle

Notes and reflections

www.ingramcontent.com/pod-product-compliance
Lightning Source LLC
Chambersburg PA
CBHW071227170526
45165CB00003B/1019